How to use t

Thank you for acquiring the *Guest Diary*! I
sure your dinner parties are always a surprise (hopefully a good one, but that's up to you)!

Table of contents

This section allows you to list all your guests and keep track of where in the diary you can find their eating habits and the history of what you have cooked for them.

Diary

Guest

Simply write in the name of the person, couple, family, or group!

Allergies & Diets

You can specify whether your guests are lactose intolerant, allergic to peanuts, vegan, etc, or whether their religion forbids certain types of food.

Likes & Dislikes

Your guest is not too keen on chicken or broccoli? Or maybe there is somebody you think shouldn't be invited at the same time? Write it here!

Other comments

For anything else you may want to mention about that guest!

The diary

We have divided it into two columns, so you can specify when you have hosted your guest and what you served on that occasion. Of course, you can add any impression and comment you want. There are 3 pages per guest, so you have enough space to record many meals in as much detail as you like!

Table of contents

Guest(s)	Page

Table of contents

Guest(s)	Page

Guest(s) : _____

Allergies and diets

Likes and dislikes

Other comments

Guest(s) : _____

Allergies and diets

Likes and dislikes

Other comments

Guest(s) : _____

Allergies and diets

Likes and dislikes

Other comments

Guest(s) : _____

Allergies and diets

Likes and dislikes

Other comments

Guest(s) : _____

Allergies and diets

Likes and dislikes

Other comments

Guest(s) : _____

Allergies and diets

Likes and dislikes

Other comments

Guest(s) : _____

Allergies and diets

Likes and dislikes

Other comments

Guest(s) : _____

Allergies and diets

Likes and dislikes

Other comments

Guest(s) : _____

Allergies and diets

Likes and dislikes

Other comments

Guest(s) : _____

Allergies and diets

Likes and dislikes

Other comments

Guest(s) : _____

Allergies and diets

Likes and dislikes

Other comments

Guest(s): _____

Allergies and diets

Likes and dislikes

Other comments

Guest(s) : _____

Allergies and diets

Likes and dislikes

Other comments

Guest(s) : _____

Allergies and diets

Likes and dislikes

Other comments

Guest(s) : _____

Allergies and diets

Likes and dislikes

Other comments

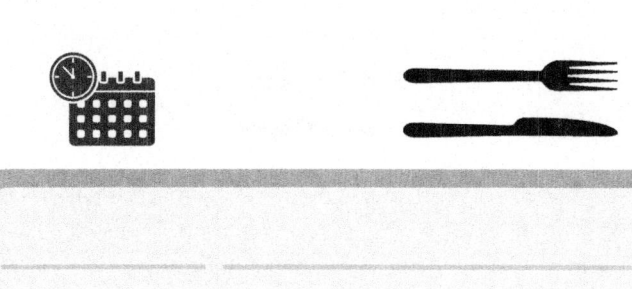

Guest(s) : _____

Allergies and diets

Likes and dislikes

Other comments

Guest(s) : _____

Allergies and diets

Likes and dislikes

Other comments

Guest(s) : _____

Allergies and diets

Likes and dislikes

Other comments

Guest(s) : _____

Allergies and diets

Likes and dislikes

Other comments

Guest(s) : _____

Allergies and diets

Likes and dislikes

Other comments

Guest(s) : _____

Allergies and diets

Likes and dislikes

Other comments

Guest(s): _____

Allergies and diets

Likes and dislikes

Other comments

Guest(s): _____

Allergies and diets

Likes and dislikes

Other comments

Guest(s) : _____

Allergies and diets

Likes and dislikes

Other comments

© seos 2020

Printed in Great Britain
by Amazon